T0065563

I Hurt and I Cry

Support for the Adult Facing the Illness of a Loved One

Dr. Cheryl A. Green

WESTBOW
PRESS®
A DIVISION OF THOMAS NELSON
& ZONDERVAN

WestBow Press books may be ordered through booksellers or by contacting:

WestBow Press
A Division of Thomas Nelson & Zondervan
1663 Liberty Drive
Bloomington, IN 47403
www.westbowpress.com
1 (866) 928-1240

ISBN: 978-1-5127-5665-4 (sc)
ISBN: 978-1-5127-5666-1 (e)

Library of Congress Control Number: 2016915135

Print information available on the last page.

WestBow Press rev. date: 09/12/2016

DEDICATION

I dedicate this book to my mother, Lottie Mae Newman,
Lawyer, who lost her battle with stomach cancer in
August of 2000, and my father, Cedric Sylvester Newman,
who died of Alzheimer's disease in August of 2011.
He was diagnosed eleven years prior to his death.

Sometimes the End of Life Comes Suddenly

As adults, we learn the unpredictability
of life through the process of living.
Friends die, spouses, siblings, and parents
die. But nothing ever prepares us when
death comes suddenly and illness is
diagnosed within the normalcy of life.

Sometimes people die when we don't expect them to.

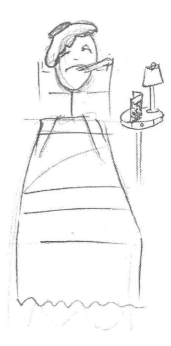

Diagnoses of cancer come without warning.
Illnesses rob us and our loved ones of wellness.
Gradually health is stolen, and
we as ask God why.

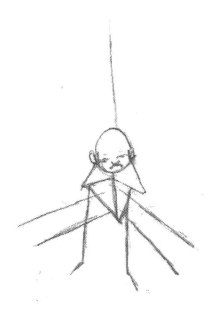

When God does not immediately respond to our questions, we feel betrayed. We ask God if he really exists. The whole world seems so dark and grim.

We feel like we can't go on.

We feel like no one will ever love
us the way our loved one did.

But God does. God loves you.
Even though your physical, emotional,
and spiritual pain is great, God
can and will comfort you.

God understands our pain.

As human beings, we seek to rationalize and understand the process of grief and mourning.

But the reality is, we just hurt, and we long to touch, smell, see, and hold our deceased loved one again.

Death seems at times to be a state
of fantasy, a fictional story.
You see, just an hour, a day, a week
ago, our loved one was alive.

Death seems unfair and callous.

Death causes the adult to feel
like a helpless child.

Lost, inconsolable, orphaned, and abandoned.

These feelings are normal and
should be expressed.
Cry and talk about how you feel to others.
It's okay to seek support.

Praying to God will help. He
will listen. He always does.

God understands our pain. He lost a Son.

Emotional, spiritual, and physical
healing will gradually come.

It is important that you eat, drink fluids, and sleep. You have experienced a loss. Death is a traumatic experience. Take care of yourself.

Permit others to love you and provide support. Sometimes it's okay to be vulnerable and ask for help.

Take a walk. Explore the simplicity of creation—sunshine, a flower, a snowflake, a tree. Feel the wind on your face.

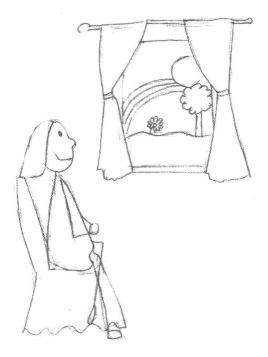

Yes, you are still alive. You have lost a loved one, but you are still here.

It is okay to give yourself permission to live.

Your heart is like a window. Sometimes it is open to the winds of life, storms push drops of heavy rains in causing damage and destruction, and yet when the rain ceases, the sun will arise again to warm us.

It is important to not be afraid to leave our hearts open to healing and forgiveness, to love and move past pain and sorrow.

People die. We will one day die.
We love, we hurt, and we love
yet again, and more.

Know that death is never an end. To believe in God is to know that a Heaven exists, and with the existence of a Heaven is hope.

We will see our deceased loved ones again. For now, we must live.

In the quiet, on your knees, close your eyes and lift your hands toward Heaven and mourn your loss. It's okay.

In the quiet, hands raised to God and kneeling in silence, ask God to give you strength to mourn, to live again despite your hurt, your pain.

God will give you the strength you need
to live beyond the grief and sorrow.

Even though I walk through the valley of the shadow of death, I will fear no evil, for you are with me; your rod and your staff, they comfort me.

—Psalm 23:4

Surely goodness and love will follow me all the days of my life, and I will dwell in the house of the Lord forever.

—Psalm 23:6

CONTEMPLATION

Who in your life is ill at this very moment?

Is your loved one's illness long-term or short-term?

Is your loved one actively dying now? If yes, who is available to provide support to him or her? Who is providing support to you?

CONTEMPLATION

Do you feel comfortable asking for
help when you are scared?

It is normal to be frightened about
being alone. What are you afraid of?

Is there someone in your life that can
provide you support? If not, consider
seeing a clergyperson or a counselor.

Consider attending a support group.
Support groups can be within hospitals,
community centers, and places of worship.

CONTEMPLATION

Spiritual support can be instrumental in your period of grief and bereavement. Sometimes clergy can better answer our spiritual questions than close friends. Consider making an appointment to discuss unresolved issues with your dying or deceased loved one.

Forgiveness is important to begin to heal. Forgive yourself, forgive the people around you, and forgive the dying or deceased person. Unforgiveness harms the person who harbors anger, bitterness, and resentment. What do you need to ask forgiveness for?

SELF-CARE

When a loved one is actively dying or has died, the grieving person often neglects his or her physical body. Ask yourself, "Am I eating enough food? Am I drinking enough fluids? Have I been able to sleep?"

Permit yourself to have some alone time. Select a place that you could go to relax. Write the name of the place below and note when you plan to go to this particular place.

Take time off from work if needed. Or, if returning to work will help you better cope with your loss, do not feel guilty— return to work. What is your decision?

Personal Notes

Personal Notes

Personal Notes

Personal Notes

Personal Notes

Personal Notes

Personal Notes

Personal Notes

BIBLIOGRAPHY

International Bible Society. *Holy Bible, New International Version.* Grand Rapids: Zondervan, 1984.

Printed in the United States
By Bookmasters